A mockingbird sings

ISBN 978-1-387-28762-8

Cover illustration: “Mockingbird”

11x14 color pencils

by

Angelaurelio Soldi 2002

To Brittany, Nathan

and

Owen

Contents

A mockingbird sings

Angelaurelio Soldi

The resources of philosophers

The day at the farm has brought no more than
the slant of light on trees,
a bright green that washes the meadows
and bird calls whether for wants or needs.
The stones sit heavy, the flesh tired,
white milk of patience threads slow time.
Then into the mix of things a small surprise.
In the shadow of oaks
two crows argue full throated.
The preposterous philosophers jab their lines,
trade back and forth noisy arguments
and their laughable strutting
and the persistence of their squabble
lighten my mood, widen the view.

Time's arrow

Inside the clock's copper case
spring loaded wheels give time its pace.
The sound visits the walls,
softens on the bookshelves open faces
and floats around the dancer's pose
set on the mantle.
Deep shadows of trees
blown by the wind
move on the Venetian blinds
and dance on the oriental carpet.
The air waits for each beat
and moves along the sound
that never alters.
Nobody is there to count.
Nobody is there to see
the wind moving the shadows,
the clock timing the trees
and the dancer keeps her pose
and on her fleeting feet
she never skips a beat.

Measuring silence

A hard rain fell all morning.
Persistent it drummed on the roof
and washed slow time away
down the scoured road
into the muddy pond,
leaving behind puddles
to landscape the yard
and a drizzle in the air.
Now all is quiet after the downpour.
I bet the heron
as he shrugs his folded wings
at the water
knows it is no time for fishing.
Dark under low clouds
trees wait and drip,
the day has grown peaceful,
craving nothing else
as it measures silence
few drops at a time.

Iris bloom

Supple, fringed laces,
fanning out lilac-colored traces,
sensuous volutes
unfolding in air
above engorged leaves
and rising upon your stalk
to lend your grace
and a fragile beauty to the garden.
You manage with elegance and ease
your delicate unfolding
while even as you bloom
your beauty already is fleeting.

An old bone

I plod along helped by yesterday's notes,
indulging what is left of old habits,
dragging, across the same days,
incertitude about facing tomorrow.
Often a dog,
barking at noises I cannot fathom.
Now and then light illuminates spaces,
rings out again and life and words
struggle to meet some purpose.
So I live also in the in-between,
careful with all that nourishes me,
a miser with my time,
a gambler at a risky game,
a clown teasing tomorrow,
an old bone leaning steadily
toward his horizon.

Mystery

A day that started in gray
suddenly breaks out,
sunshine flooding the meadows,
no two blades alike.
The magic of sunlight
lifts every shade out of every color,
its magic like the magic
of mockingbirds' songs
electrifying the air.
I walk in it and it is clear now
yesterday did not matter,
the day has come
to fill my heart and I
was not even ready.

I know trees that keep their mind

The trees on my farm fill up my eyes,
sing their songs in colors.
I am they say and so are you.
They have no reason to lie,
long after I am gone they will be here,
that too explains their insolence
and the indifference they display when they surprise.
They stand, not compromised by words,
doing whatever they have learned to do
to profit from the soil and every rain.
The time will come for them to recon,
never knowing for sure
when their branches will crash
under the weight of ice
or bend more under more weight and time.
At the wood boundary I keep a clean edge
in deference to my love of meadows,
it says as much about my stubbornness
as it say about their reach
to shade and grow across that line.
I do not threaten the rest of their domain,
where I like to roam.
I think I am fair but I don't know
for when I visit they always keep their mind.

Confabulating frogs

When in my walks I skirt the pond,
no sooner have I approached, one will dive,
expanding waves its only trace.
And in the evening if I reach the wood,
ahead of me the chorus line falls silent.
Cautious peepers, confabulating frogs,
come dark I'll overhear their gossip
drift across the meadows grasses.
They cannot change their ways with me
any more that they can change their skin,
inheritors of millions of years,
over our short acquaintance time
they struggle to survive the poisoned world I make.
Graduates of the school that spans water and air,
they enjoy the borderline and there spill croaking voices
with what contentment only they know.
Philosophers of the pause,
awake beneath somnolent eyes,
they listen for a mate in each answering call.
And they are wise in the rotundity of their belly,
waiting for meals to come their way
or floating half submerged to spy.
Hopping ponderously from place to place,
unhurriedly they inhabit and complete my landscape,
weaving together theirs and other lives,
sending to my porch petulant refrains
to frame reassuringly the other sounds that fill my life.

A mockingbird sings

After an absence
I have come again to the river,
to the sculpted banks,
the overhang of trees,
the strewn rocks skirted by whirlpools
and the flat flow,
quiet along sandy shallows.
After its labors
driftwood rests
just above the water line.
Here where the bank rises
and the river flows,
the sky touches down
breathing in the threes
where spoken words fade into silence.
A mockingbird sings.
The river flow carries the song
and the memories of summers past,
measuring time in soft whispers
and slow gulps no words can master.

Call me when you have found the key

There are mischievous days
turning routine sightings into visions,
invading the mind, jolting the heart.
They invent possibilities,
advertise revolutions,
not just novelties
to bring about pleasant times.
Then the mind goes to work
wears its lab coat, says adagio,
don’t wreck the order
in which things are found.
Adventures, we know, fling the heart,
some lucky one bring joy,
most only dream at the start.
And the day has no answers,
sits remiss on the floor,
it has brought no faith,
nor a key to unlock the door.

Squatters

They honk on approach.
First, isolated trumpets sound off the landing,
then a chattering breaks out as they veer and bank
toward the pond's surface,
spreading out their legs, webbing their landing gears,
dangling fat bellies on the last currents of air.
With a cacophony of voices upon splash down
they cheer the leading pilot and shake their wings
before they settle down.
Honk-wise they can quietly chatter after they explore the pond,
search the grasses, drop waste and preen their feathers
while their sentinels' malevolent eye follows intruders.
I hear their squabbles but don't understand the mind of geese.
In their slow studied walk they spread out on the land
as if they own the neighborhood.
They grudgingly yield my right of way
and squatted on my meadow, by my pond
they follow me on my walks with suspicious eyes.
They remind me of diffident peasant women,
large, sitting cross armed in front of their doors,
after supper, having done their chores,
studiously watching a stranger go by.

Free at last

Sss…ii..lll…vvii..aaa.
Incredulous the letters labor
off the pen onto the page
guided by a careful hand,
slow along that first trace.
Then Silvia stands,
smiles,
recognizes her name
and feels free
for the first time
at eighty-five.

Land of New Mexico

Red bloodied oxides of your birthing, layered and fractured,
deep gouged and silt engorged land of time past and still forming
I see you burdened with the mountains of your heavy hefting,
I survey you dressed by the patient layering
of ancient running waters,
strewn with the ruins
of the burning rivers roaring up from your belly.
I think of you land forming in an ocean of space,
gathered in a universe full of emptiness,
not yet prone to life, not yet green under a living blanket.
The astonishing history of your layers,
the catalogue of bones, of the many lives you sheltered,
here where you gathered to start this story,
in these harsh arroyos where you question and confuse me.
Here where your womb speaks of your labors
I am aghast,
reduced by your wilderness, by your bright air,
by the unfathomable depths of your brooding purposes
and lastly soothed
by the becalming presence of your vast laid out mesas.

Entering Acoma

I descend into Acoma's bowl,
a cathedral of air and light
encircled by the rocks of a vast design.
Everywhere the space is ancient
and ancient is its time.
It would seem harsh to die here
surrounded by this beauty,
under the mystery of its skies
and one can see how here
the mind must have started to play
confronted with the puzzles
in the rocks of this display.
Here surely God was invented
to soothe the gaping soul
when beneath these Herculean walls
man felt alone and small.
I feel I am on a pilgrimage,
in awe on entering this space,
suffering its inexplicable draw
as I climb the currents of its air
that lift my thought
and cannot rest it anywhere.
Under this vast eternity, I am sure,
prayers must have been born at last
in souls scorched by its beauty,
in hearts this landscape held fast.

Place of gatherings

Wind and rocks
talk to each other
above the pines.
Frijoles canyon,
gatherer of people,
shelter for homes.
The creek sings to the birches
and listen to the raven's cry.
Frijoles canyon,
shelter for homes,
place of gatherings
and time.

A world bereft.

A world bereft of its libraries,
its first temples, mosques and cathedrals;
a world were no laboratory hums,
no orchestra plays the vibrant air,
shorn of images or plays
such a world would be almost
as strange and inhospitable to me
as one bereft of its forests,
the clear voices of its rivers,
the solitude of its mountains,
empty of birds giving chase in the air.
It would be inhospitable like
a sea abandoned by its waters
or a hamlet deserted, hearing no voices,
witnessing no rituals pacing the day.
Words and images born out of ordinary days,
music played at the rhythm of life,
fed by shared needs, nourished by surprises
and first discoveries.
Words and music, temples and images
ideas born, again and again,
and left undiminished despite our arrogance
have made, make and sustain my world.
They are the company among which I live,
feel alive, comforted, bewildered.

A mess in my garden

Fall sleeps in the wood these nights
and day after day changes its colors;
only yesterday its friend the wind visited
tossing about bloody reds and rusty yellows.
But the fool doesn't know how to gather the wind
even less how to use its many brushes
and desperate throws up his arms
randomly painting
now the trees then even the bushes.
The crow, with his charlatan voice,
laughs at him almost splitting his belly,
while chatty squirrels busy gather nuts
which in their dreams at night they tally.
Deer eat their way through the last berries
and mockingbirds go searching for more,
undaunted only the oaks stay put,
having seen all that mess many times before.

Figs

Under the parched skies of this year hot summer
my fig tree patiently bears sun-braided morsel
of honey-laced sweetness.
Gifts I savor. They bring ripening memories,
bridge boundaries of time.
Lanes lined with bushes of ripening figs,
sun bathed rocks, sun drenched sea.
In my eyes your brightness,
sunburn on my skin and
sliding off my arms warm waters.
A strong life rising in my veins,
I am a fish in your currents,
my head cleaving the salty surface,
my eye level to the horizon
and in my wake hardly any presence.
Immersed in your vastness,
suspended above your terrifying darkness,
I am alive in your depth
and hear your song of wind and waves and air,
gifts that in my mind even now I harvest.
Splayed, under the sun upon your sands
again I hear your lambent voice,
happy in my tiredness.
Waters that freed me,
harsh even the sun's shadows
and on my lips salt,
lacing the sweet and heavy pulp of summer.

Night of the fishing moon

The hazelnut moon
has come to fish my pond.
She sits on a bank of clouds
drops her baited hook and waits.
It is the fishes dreaming hour.
Sleepy, they have not slept
since last the whippoorwill came
singing them into their dreams,
they don't know about tomorrow.
They are too tired and like the dry creek,
exhausted, they have sunk to the bottom.
Algae float, heavy on my pond
and the moon can't see its bottom.
Go away hazelnut moon!
Come back when you are silver
and cast at least a glimmer
of wonder over the meadow.
Until you brighten the pond's face
they have nothing more to give my fishes,
then write new dreams on their silent eyes,
and brighten their sleepy scales.

Tire tracks

I come across tire tracks
in one of which a frog lies. Flattened.
A life has come to its end,
a frog mind run out of time,
a most physical image in the mud
of my own state of mind.
Despite my soothing pace
the sounds of woodland's life surrounding,
in my mind time is not advancing.
In a corner the pond's surface is frothing,
I do not stop to explore.
Close to the spring a white flower,
where white lilies used to grow,
I see but do not go.
I am oblivious to what is changing,
out but not in the flow
and the signs I gather do not interest me.
My mind is ill at ease, spinning in place,
ignoring pesky crows chatting the news,
on a walk having nowhere to go,
just like that poor frog said a while ago.

Maybe God doesn't care

So much rests on chance and place.
Some enjoy ham that is lean
other do not dare or chance
to dream ham in their dreams.

When are we going to haven? Ha?
Why do we have to endure?
Few of us have the *stamen*, ha?
Fewer have a *sine cure*.

Nothing is fair. Not ever!
Some always speak and spout,
other though they are *cleverer*
their chances are only *remout*.

Why aren't we going to Haven?
That's what I want to know,
misery comes seven by seven
I want so much to go.

She said: My love for you is golden.
I bought her a golden band
and though to me *bethrolden*
gave it to her lover friend.

I want to go to Haven
where there is love for all,

where to each one is given
to have good *insouls*.

When are we going to Haven?
To lift the angel's skirts,
see if their legs are even
or if one comes up short.

I do not know my dear,
I do not know my dear,
maybe God doesn't care,
that's why we are stuck down here.

The reason why

I watched young men jump off high, sheer mountain faces,
open their suit-webbed arms and dive like birds in flight
to feel life, invincible in the streaming air.
I told my wife: that is what I want to do.
She said: you are crazy.
I am not afraid, I thought,
though, even if I were not afraid
I know I'll never do it anyhow.
Could be poetry is my poor substitute for living,
for what I couldn't do or did not dare.
Maybe that is why I am restless,
pretend they are confident my days
while I try to stiffen my shoulders
under the weight of indifferent,
unyielding skies.

To my daphnia twig on its first blooming

Daphnia, deep breathing,
abandoning yourself
to hills and woodlands,
eloquent with green,
today Spring visited you,
love-shy you,
shepherdess of windy tunes,
nourished by streams.
Forsaking love's strife,
yet not in fear
but verdant in living,
you distill the secret,
pungent, sweetness
of your essence
to fill today with joy
my window.

A break in the clouds

Today we had a break in the weather,
a small sun thinning the clouds,
rather like a poem timidly trying to surface
from among its words,
freeing itself and returning after a long exile.
I took advantage of it
noticing all the things it was not saying,
all the details left out
and the distracting way the sun was hesitating
and never quite removed the clouds.
After days alone with words
had brought stalemate and exhaustion
I felt this was some respite
and tomorrow I would only have myself to fear,
my hesitation to scrap legless words,
gain precious time.

Mimmi

There is a woman I liked,
I mean she truly was my friend.
In her a child survived
who called me forth
to laugh and to play.
She was a gentle presence,
simplicity in her smile as she faced patiently
what harshness came her way.
I loved to cook meals with her,
a plain fare
and at her table to navigate from rough seas
to placid village shores
and I don't care to remember
the pain I felt when untimely she died.
I loved the time she spent with me,
memories and feelings
my heart will not let go.

My daughters' friend

Often in my mind I still watch you,
each day singing another verse of your song,
some sadness in your voice betraying
your mother's days, the son you lost.
My mind is still visiting the memories
of gentle days and the company you brought to us.
Water and flour on the kitchen counter,
my two daughters' small hands at work,
your broad smile hovering over their labors,
their giggles as they squish the dough.
Then, as the aroma of bread
from the oven is wafting into our day,
the stories told to two little girls
glad that this evening at last you wouldn't go.
Often denying your heavy heart
you brought ease to our living,
the clarity of your being, simple and true,
your warmth in giving without pretentious art.

One must hope

Under these late autumnal glows
I will rinse my soul
not virginal but almost clean.
I'll welcome and find soothing
cooler days and quieter skies,
clear out the porch mend the rock wall.
Fewer pretenses about vigor in the past,
less gloom of future doom
and I'll invent a little, if I can,
but I'll accept clichés, some are fundamental.
Like before there will be many,
buried in novelties or the next adventure.
Now and then I'll take leave of my sanity,
for hope springs eternal,
then return as I must to my landscape.
It will be there to welcome me,
the golden prison I like and know so well.
Perhaps in days to come it will offer more,
more needed shelter.
Perhaps kind words even in old clichés
will ease the march of Medicare time
and weave into the calendar of seasons
a brave new hope.

New life

To Brittany and Nathan on their Wedding, August 13, 2016

Who without hesitation would say
this little girl, that little boy?
Tottering steps, tiny shrill voices.
Only a fool would say without hesitation
this little girl, that little boy.
A last chirp and evenings ease out,
on the last croak evenings are sealed
and always suns turn their wheels,
rise and reveal the many schooled lives
of girls and boys.
Only a fool would pretend
to recognize the same old story.
Notes ring out in thousands different songs,
bodies ripen, adventures beckoning somewhere,
minds expand into the possibilities of youthful time.
Not knowing, sap rises and goes to work,
to feed the leaves, make the world green,
grow the supple forms that grace the trees
and on the hills of springs,
through harvests of summer days,
a young man, a young woman walk
confident, proud,
not knowing yet and then somehow
finding each other, falling in love.
Maybe none but an old fool can say
the storms they'll weather, the peace they'll earn
as they will learn to love.

The heart generous when pleased
but stubborn still, wanting its way.
Though not even an old fool can tell
all the strange miracles and joys
of which are capable their hearts,
for we have seen their promises,
now witness their desire to share together life
and shout their happiness into the sky,
as grateful we rejoice
because they have brought to us new life.

Prudent the wind

Prudent the wind moves across the meadow
carrying the seeds of much that is to grow
it doesn't plan its course nor knows its law,
where goes its treasure only the furrows know.

A scrim of falling drops moves over the wood
alike it travels and falls across the field
parching the thirst of land ready to yield
feeding the creek there where the heron stood.

Life under the steady pulse of seasons
visits its clients, dispersing diligently its store,
cradling newborns, grown-ups challenging more,
full of suspense, rich with surprises, giving no reasons.

Last years' tracks once more are overrun,
promises are laid out and energies are spent
battles resume and flowers redolent with scent
again open up new petals in turning to the sun.

Blue birds

When my blue birds spread their wings
it is as if they are flashing joy,
falling in and out of the sky.
If from the house I catch a glimpse of them,
I move from window to window
to see them chase each other, acrobats in the air.
Noticing what light does on their plumage
is only half the pleasure,
they are gamblers after new tricks,
rustling, stealing each other game.
A restless lot when around,
even the trees seem to stand still just to stare.
The other birds don't entertain half as much,
unlike the blue birds they mostly eat at my feeder.
Under trees, in the woods I pile cut bushes, fallen limbs
maybe they will use them for shelters,
in winter when I can't find them.
Often I have watched one
looking out from his perch on a branch
before he flits away
and I have wandered what is he planning
or does the play comes natural to him.
They hardly seem to notice me
or only when I move,
perhaps they are aware I cannot fly,
maybe the know I am heavy.

Days when I was young

I sit gazing at the fields.
Today my silly heart aches
on so much that went by.
The day is ending and there was
no time then, no urgency
among endless distractions,
youth vigorous and braying.
And now the day is ending.
Threads of past times, lost energies
and longings
inflate memories.
I look into the distance.
In my mind's eye,
along the sweep of the woods,
like distracted passersby,
drift the things I remember,
the grasses growing,
darker in the setting light.

If only storks could deliver

The orgy of power or the madness of sanctity?
Which is to be feared more?
For want of grace to abuse the body
or cripple the ambitious mind for want of power.
Which is the worst to bear?
The saintly Thomas Moore?
Or larger than life Henry the VIII?
Shall we crush or murder those who stand
in the way of our power?
Shall we torture those who challenge
our views of God?
It is as if the storks have dropped their babies
and we know nothing of how they have been bred.
But we have known the bloodshed before the saintly glory
and we have witnessed the robbery on which power is set.
Guided by power mainly or entirely by God redeemed
always and just as miserably our lives have been misled.
If only storks could deliver more than by man is bred.

Having it nature's way.

On my farm I don't plant nor do I build.
Whatever I can mow I call it grass
and in the flower beds or along edges
I only weed when invasive growth
disparages the established view.
I enjoy the generous profusion in the woods,
sharing its rightful order, in resourceful places
finding pause in intimate seclusion.
Shrubs and trees balance out their use of space,
competing lives, different species finding
beneficial ways to thrive.
To the deer the squirrels, coons, snakes, blue birds,
cardinals and jays must be natural neighbors.
The land sometime is stressed and always is visited by trials
but survives and prospers when it can,
opportunist with what it takes, efficient in using what it needs.
It doesn't need my work to improve its act
nor do I have any desire to attempt that,
fortunately I don't need to profit.
I have cleared some pastures,
to rest my eyes upon their gentle slopes
and I have contrived to keep loneliness away
when looking at that restful view and even feel some pride,
noticing my work, especially its restraint.
Not everyone is privileged to bask in Nature's ways,
to find in it most of what he needs
as I find most every day.

A crow cries.

I enter the wood where
the summer colors already are muted
and almost naked branches lift themselves
to reach out to the sky.
A glossy layer covers the forest floor,
drizzle misting the air,
coating leaves, enveloping me.
The poplars rise tall,
solitary against a cowing sky,
in the distance a crow screeches
then silence.
Nothing moves on the forest floor,
nothing between the trees,
stillness fills the air
with a quiet melancholy that finds
and comforts me.

Flowerpot windows

Tittle-tattle souls, gentle gossiping partners,
each in turn a target and happy to stitch our voices
onto the daily trivia that mark our ways.
We ask no more than to be heard
and now and then forgiven
for what we cannot but routinely do
or ought to do and then don't do
and file away.
Little houses with flowerpot windows,
hearts open to joy, learning to trade
more laughter, still harbor hope
and shrug off dead time.
Then when we turn around
some Wednesday or Sunday
we can only wonder at all that has gone bye
and seemed just another day.
Tittle-tattle souls
full of longings and sympathy
for days of easy living which not long ago
we somehow could muster.

Fartwell

When I heard he had died
under my breath I said *fartwell.*
He had an inordinate propensity and ability
to quietly let loose, sometimes,
regardless of place and time,
and by look and guile
to redirect the blame
on the one full of it
he disapproved of.
He compensated by being someone
with a deep understanding of wine,
offering not florid characterizations
but frequent and thoughtful invitations to share.
He saw clearly and was adamant that
there was no generosity in anyone
who insisted on sharing a sober mind.
Not one to complain nor did he whine,
adversity as good a challenge as sunshine,
pass the bottle let's make this a pleasant time.
Pronouncements, they were few,
he hated to pretend he knew what to say
or what to do. He made unpretentiously
his way through life.
A sharp, yes a cynical mind
but, not only when drinking,
a generous heart,
his glass was full: How about yours?

Jack-rabbit April

Jack-rabbit April already is leaving us behind!
After long-toothed winter's somber light
Finally there were light-shafts bright enough to blind

And dancing blooms working on our mind
But as we look surprised at birds in flight
Jack-rabbit April is already leaving us behind.

Meadows filled with flowers of every kind,
New greens tassel the land and fill our sight
And light-shafts bright enough to blind

Dress birds with colors and alert our minds
So we too feel as if we could take flight.
Alas jack-rabbit April already left us behind.

In warmer May is useless to try to find
A sharpness that fills the world as might
April's light-shafts bright enough to blind.

Come to light a spark in sleeping minds
First with his rains and then his birds in flight
Jack-rabbit April left us and no one can find
His light-shafts bright enough to blind.

Most of my sunsets have gathered

Had I wisdom I'd share it with you
but I have only facts,
lemon rinds after the lemonade
and though I wish I could tell you
pray to your God for your pleasures,
God doesn't work that way,
you must sin for your pleasures,
ask forgiveness after you are caught.
I have watched many sunsets
for some hidden message, maybe a nod.
All of them quivered, all left behind an empty sky,
night closing in absentmindedly,
darkness wasting no time.
Only when on my walks
the opening of a flower,
tracks along the creek's bank
or the company of stars
tell me I am not alone,
how I have learned from my body
and, luckily, how I have made myself a home,
only then I stop.
Yes, I stop wasting my feelings
on much to me still unknown.

Nose to the ground

Early on a Saturday morning,
in the predawn slumber of trees and sky,
my daughter's dog on a leash
pulls me along our country lane,
finding his way, nose to the ground.
From the faint outline of trees across the pond
comes the chirping of a bird starting his morning.
Clear your throat and the cobwebs of sleep,
spin your philosophy for the day that's starting,
we don't know what it will be like
but we start it in your company
in this comfortable silence, its soft darkness.
Down the lane I hear your trailing off voice
broadcast among silent shapes under the sky
and I am reassured, the dog knows its way,
the sun rises to awake our neighborhood.

Pulling weeds

Not sure how to proceed
I have left my desk for the garden,
there are always weeds to clean out.
They pull out easily after yesterday rain.
While I work this birds says pee, pee, pee,
all the time.
The sun is worm on my shoulders,
my hands are searching underneath lilies,
around irises and beneath peonies.
Pee, pee, pee he keeps up all the time,
pee, pee, pee no one responding.
The other birds mind their own voices.
Pee, pee, pee again and again no one responding.
Finally I give up and move inside the house,
annoyed, even irritated
that someone with a brain
much smaller than mine
should display so much self-confidence.

Set in the wild

Poplars shooting up, straight, oaks branching out, wide,
hawthorns' dark-spiked leaves clustering, lustrous,
sycamores in tortuous attire,
supple loblolly pines with brushes of needles, painting,
pungent ciders deep in blue berries trade,
umbrellas of black walnuts, dappling the lawn
and hickory's furious crowns
harbor my school,
mark my stately in place wood held confines.
Necessity and rain grow their lines,
Quiet, filtered light nurtures their seasons.
At their bases dead branches,
broken limbs scattered by storms,
higher up scars that a patient bark is slowly closing.
Necessity again roots them and they grip the ground,
rounding boulders and stones
to sink into the earth and drink under the rains.
Squirrels harvest and distribute their nuts,
in the fall winds layer their leaves on the ground
that time will turn into loam.
Woodpeckers clean their bark
while in Spring a riot of leaves again will harvest suns.
The delicate greens they bring to life each year
are they so originally composed
because they don't remember the last season?
The harmony of their outstretched branches is so assured.
By the creek a turkey left a feather,
under the willow oaks lay deer droppings and acorn shells.

Strong trees sheltering lives.
An old giant buttresses his trunk
and grows more wood into stronger limbs
where greeter strain requires more.
Resilience shaping long lives
that have no need of measuring time. .
Not words just whispers carried by a breeze,
and roars when storms bear down on their crowns.
Is the abundance of their foliage cause for their air of joy?
Set in the wild where necessity is pure my woods prosper,
each year they endure.

There

It is there
and I can see it.
Early at down,
each morning,
quietly, it leaves
from the edge of the dark wood,
a sloping curve that on the pasture
silently reaches to the pond
as morning ends night repose.
Many days I walk there
and then there are weeks
I never go.
But I know
it is there.

The metaphors of the heart

The history and adventures of the heart
play such a central role and have plenty of clout
for a small pump chugging on diligently
until it finally gives out.
The heart knows so many feelings and variety of parts,
in playbills the mind enrich with words,
though it is generally known
the heart only speeds up
or else slows down.
All over the body is where
one comes across merciless urges,
the heart only catches up
when, inconsiderate, one takes a plunge
or else the heart take up more somber timing
when one is fooled or tired of trying.
Commiserated, invoked, praised,
extolled for strength
or for cowardice berated
and yet the heart never changes notes,
it merely races a bit or else slows down
just to be adequate.

Worn out

It is not unusual when poets start to gripe
to harp on gross materialism in all its forms and stripes,
though that is nothing new nor is it much to fear,
except it's advertised so loud to warp out hears.
In past ages there was much less to own and hold,
people spending their time to overcome hunger and cold,
so it isn't so bad that now to comfort we aspire,
much worst is that we waste what now is easier to acquire.

At times we poets gripe on a world alienated from true art,
for art, we believe, makes a human an animal apart.
But art has always been a rarity of a bird,
the call of few never the aim of the stampeding heard.
The rich have always bought art to dress up their fame,
the poor have seen God dressed in art to bless His name,
but while it's true that far too many pass their wits for art
it's even truer that many more now cultivate it in their hearts.

And if in horror we poets lament the violence of our days,
shaken by the cruelty and gore that life and fantasy display,
we can't ignore the epics upon the defeated we erected,
the bodies and souls we sang, who conquered then subjected.
Poets decry the lack of hesitation to rape and exterminate,
just as there seem to be no end to bigotry and hate,
why not be encouraged that now on every shore at last
some fight for human rights and to redress the past?

Yes too often it is harsh and vile this world
as much as it was vile before, so we are told.
Each generation in turn must relearn to rise
above ignorance and greed, learn again to despise
the brutal selfish lust for power and for gold,
move beyond the boundaries of fear and bold
strike out for peace, for decency, for hope
accept the truth of death, of life fathom the scope.

You might think it naïve to put a cheerful spin
on a bloodied world of people driven to fight and win
and you may see dilettantism only as sign of more decline,
since you may conceive of art as something most sublime
or you may fancy yourself a hero all alone,
given so many of us stay comfortably ensconced at home,
but what am I to do with all of poets' gripe and sadness?
I must find hope. I am just a thin sheet this side of madness.

Now

Young, now you carry
effortlessly
assurance and cheerfulness
in your voice.
In your eyes
there is no wear or fear.
Everything to you is new
and you are eager
every time you try.
I know,
I was that young too.

Scaling the tower of Babel

Having grown to shape our times,
the language of our thinking puts us at the center
though much still escapes our brow.
I want to know what chickadees are thinking
and the hawk inveterate fierceness
from where does it takes its view?
The languages of the frogs I want to hear,
I want to understand the calls
that in the evenings ring the pond.
Who without further prying can trust his inklings
when it comes to crickets' songs?
The messages guarded by the stones?
The upheaval among the stars?
Even if it were haphazardly,
how butterflies think concerns me too.
And how the cadence repeats
that brings along each season,
in multihued languages how it sounds
soft, harsh, subtle, resounding.
How it hides, later to surprise,
become joy as much as harbinger of pain.
Mysteries that grip the heart,
bewilder restless minds, let alone souls
on the rocky shoreline of thought.

The child that was

Light sometimes comes, finds us chastised.
Souls appended to lives of sunken griefs and muted joys.
Then another light comes, scatters softly
and barely filters through low set clouds
ending in a haze smoothing all edges.
Morning and we, we sober out,
longing for rest not for another day,
the drudgery and the dead end thoughts
of languages we had to learn
after the thrills of the small child we used to be
and in that washed out light
the child's voice rings
and a strange nostalgia settles like joy
behind closed eyes,
seeing again like the first time.

Silent mountains

Harbingers of progress is what we think we are,
mastering adversity, abstracting Nature's laws.
But are we not propagandists waging profitable wars
overwhelming a world we have just begun to know?

We gather scores of facts to buttress our deeds,
the health and comforts some of us enjoy become proofs
and those we use but find themselves in need
we assure will only benefit when we enlarge our roofs.

Nature thrives on balance and in every virgin space
weaves together function and beauty in magical designs
but not where restlessly we assert our pace,
where our greed and ego we cannot restrain.

Our minds are apt to learn but still we cannot tame our hearts,
stubborn and sold on arrogance and self-deceits.
We have faiths, opinions and cultures, use them to tear us apart
and overlooking waste and plunder march to our defeat.

The rage of our offended souls or the sweet moments of fear
when we are startled or stung by some despair,
when in our hearts and minds an opening is struggling to appear,
often we call exaggerations to which we shouldn't lend our ear.

The hard to learn and hard to hold onto serenity and joy
of simpler lives and more enlightened ways

we dismiss them as nostalgia of immature boys,
toying with delusions that should be best put away.

But one by one, like flakes of snow, yellow leaves will fall
against backdrops of stately pines
and again will maple's sap be ruled by seasons' call
and in the distance, silent mountains watch, drawing their lines.

And in the silence one can hear them call.

The cemetery at Cavtat

I reach the hilltop and enter a garden
surrounded by a slender wood of pines,
sloping to the shore below
lapped by a lazy sea.
The notables lay in the chapel,
others rest under funerary steles and urns,
lining alleys on the summit among evergreens.
On the gentler slope,
where the wood opens to the sea,
the rest all lay under marble.
I have come, visiting, a stranger.
By the chapel's door, quietly,
an old woman dressed in black
sells mementoes and laces
in the patterns my mother knitted
and laid on furniture,
under the silver, crystal vases,
and statuettes of her silent house.
Silent like the houses that here climb
the other side of this hill,
bougainvillea draped over garden walls
over which also the fig tree arches.
Small yards of penumbra and shadows,
entries to disciplined lives,
where inside the still air barely answers
the pendulum clock chime,
while in the filtered light bathing the walls

hang familiar faces
who here lived their patient lives.
In one arch I see our lives inhabit
the solitude of this hilltop silence.

The armchair in the parlor

Were have the hours gone?
The sharp morning hours,
the days that rode into evening on strong shoulders,
the ordinary filling each ordinary day
and the strange and unexpected surprises
for which the pendulum kept time,
patiently, in the hall.
The armchair, its arms worn out,
waits in the parlor
and on the porch few scattered shoes.
One asks but really expects no answer,
just the same one asks.
Yesterday went silently
like a tide leaving its flotsam.
One asks, not knowing exactly
what was expected,
not knowing what failed to come
one asks just the same.

I get little help from my neighbors

I know mostly oaks, ciders, loblolly pines
and sycamores sinuously growing,
olive, brown and white.
They all rise out of red clay,
a native soils unlike my own,
new like the ways and sounds,
one learns under a different light and sky.
Crows jabbering in the neighborhood,
their wobbling, plodding gate,
as if entitling them to every acre,
so unlike the peaceful grazing of the deer.
The blue jays razzmatazz is not much help
as I seek quiet to sort out the last few years
and the persnickety look of elusive raccoons,
that I have not seen recently, wouldn't make things any clearer.
Scurrying, mindless squirrels are plenty,
though they add little more than holes and quarrels
when I am about harboring hesitations and some fears.
Only the dogwoods branches, swaying low
can be relied on to harmonize the view.
One moves with the seasons, uncertainly so,
reasons to marvel are everywhere and abundant,
the occasions to drift pleasantly always near
but days here and there crumble
when the same questions arise
that seemed promising at twenty.

When morning raises sabers

When morning raises sabers of light
not everything and not every heart awakes.
The sun shines its light
gradually filling out darkness
and then moves on
like a mindless drunkard spilling its wine
while routine business overtakes each mind
and though moving from house to house
the sun invents always new lights,
another day is wasted on sleepwalkers
too busy to see how full above them
the day rides.

Too simple to be true

Trained as a scientist
more than once I have been asked
how come I am writing poems,
to which I have replayed:
each of my daughters
gave me a notebook once
and invited me to fill it up.
They have since
given me more notebooks.
People don't believe me.
May be they think
poetry needs much more
than simple presents.
I am not sure myself
what poetry needs
and I have stopped telling people
why I am writing poems,
struggling to fill up notebooks.

Where the light ends

Deep shadows,
still,
smooth-lying,
clear,
gathered,
sharper than the bright light
lining your edges,
pool of quietness
drawing me in
to rest
and to hope.

www.ingramcontent.com/pod-product-compliance
Ingram Content Group UK Ltd.
Pitfield, Milton Keynes, MK11 3LW, UK
UKHW041919190726
13854UKWH00003B/1326

9 781387 287628